AF226183

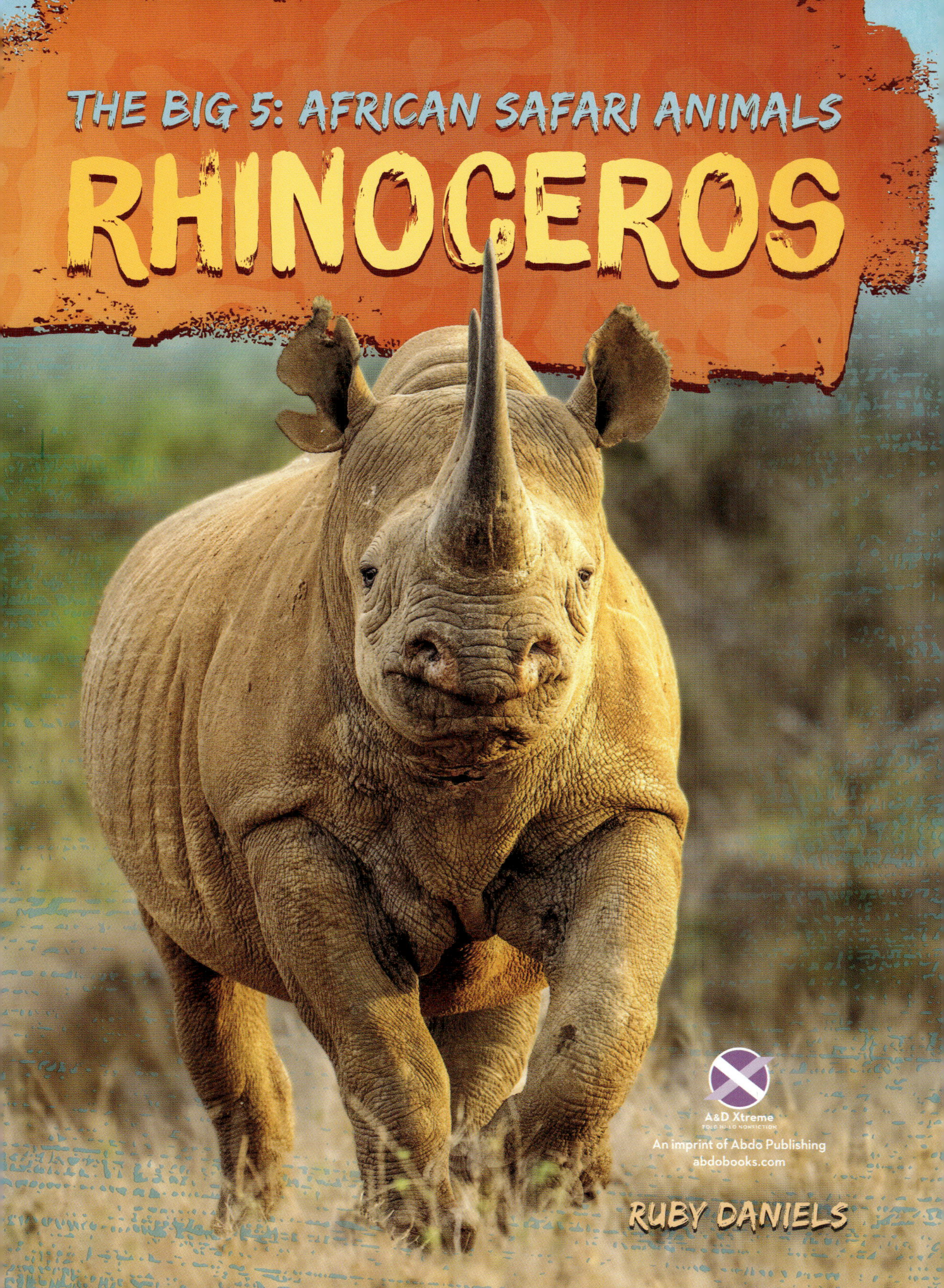

THE BIG 5: AFRICAN SAFARI ANIMALS
RHINOCEROS
A&D Xtreme
An imprint of Abdo Publishing
abdobooks.com
RUBY DANIELS

TAKE IT TO THE XTREME!

GET READY FOR AN EXTREME ADVENTURE!
THE PAGES OF THIS BOOK WILL TAKE YOU INTO
THE THRILLING WORLD OF ICONIC AFRICAN ANIMALS.
WHEN YOU HAVE FINISHED READING THIS BOOK, TAKE THE
XTREME CHALLENGE ON PAGE 45 ABOUT WHAT YOU'VE LEARNED!

ABDOBOOKS.COM

Published by Abdo Publishing, a division of ABDO, PO Box 398166, Minneapolis, Minnesota 55439.
Copyright © 2026 by Abdo Consulting Group, Inc. International copyrights reserved in all countries.
No part of this book may be reproduced in any form without written permission from the publisher.
A&D Xtreme™ is a trademark and logo of Abdo Publishing.
Printed in the United States of America, North Mankato, MN.
052025
092025

THIS BOOK CONTAINS
RECYCLED MATERIALS

Design: Kelly Doudna, Mighty Media, Inc.
Production: Mighty Media, Inc.
Editor: Katherine Chu

Cover Photograph: nwdph/Shutterstock

Interior Photographs: annabelle07/Shutterstock, pp. 12–13; Beate Wolter/Shutterstock, pp. 22–23; Ben Curtis/AP Images, pp. 42–43; Chris Twine/Shutterstock, pp. 4–5; Gunter Nuyts/Shutterstock, pp. 14–15; Jen Watson/Shutterstock, pp. 26–27; Lance van de Vyver/Shutterstock, pp. 20–21; Lynn Yeh/Shutterstock, pp. 34–35; nwdph/Shutterstock, p. 1; Peter Bruins/Shutterstock, pp. 24–25; Photo by Christopher S/Shutterstock, pp. 6–7; Pixelbykev/Shutterstock, pp. 30–31; Reto Buehler/Shutterstock, pp. 28–29; Roger de la Harpe/Shutterstock, p. 9; Rudi Hulshof/Shutterstock, pp. 38–39; Shams F Amir/Shutterstock, pp. 18–19; Simon Eeman/Shutterstock, pp. 32–33; Som Moulick/Shutterstock, pp. 16–17; Timo Alejandro Steiner/Shutterstock, p. 8; Tyrone Winfield/Shutterstock, pp. 36–37; Udo Kieslich/Shutterstock, pp. 40–41; Vaclav Sebek/Shutterstock, pp. 10–11; Wirestock/iStockphoto, p. 44

Design Elements: DGIM studio/Adobe Stock (distressed texture); Ografica/Adobe Stock (header background); Zebra Finch/Adobe Stock (header background)

LIBRARY OF CONGRESS CONTROL NUMBER: 2024948576
PUBLISHER'S CATALOGING-IN-PUBLICATION DATA
Names: Daniels, Ruby, author.
Title: Rhinoceros / by Ruby Daniels
Description: Minneapolis, Minnesota : Abdo Publishing, 2026 | Series: The big 5: African safari animals | Includes online resources and index.
Identifiers: ISBN 9781098296346 (lib. bdg.) | ISBN 9798384917779 (ebook)
Subjects: LCSH: Rhinoceroses--Juvenile literature. | Endangered animals--Juvenile literature. | Big game animals--Africa--Juvenile literature. | Herbivores--Juvenile literature. | Safaris--Juvenile literature.
Classification: DDC 591.96--dc23

CONTENTS

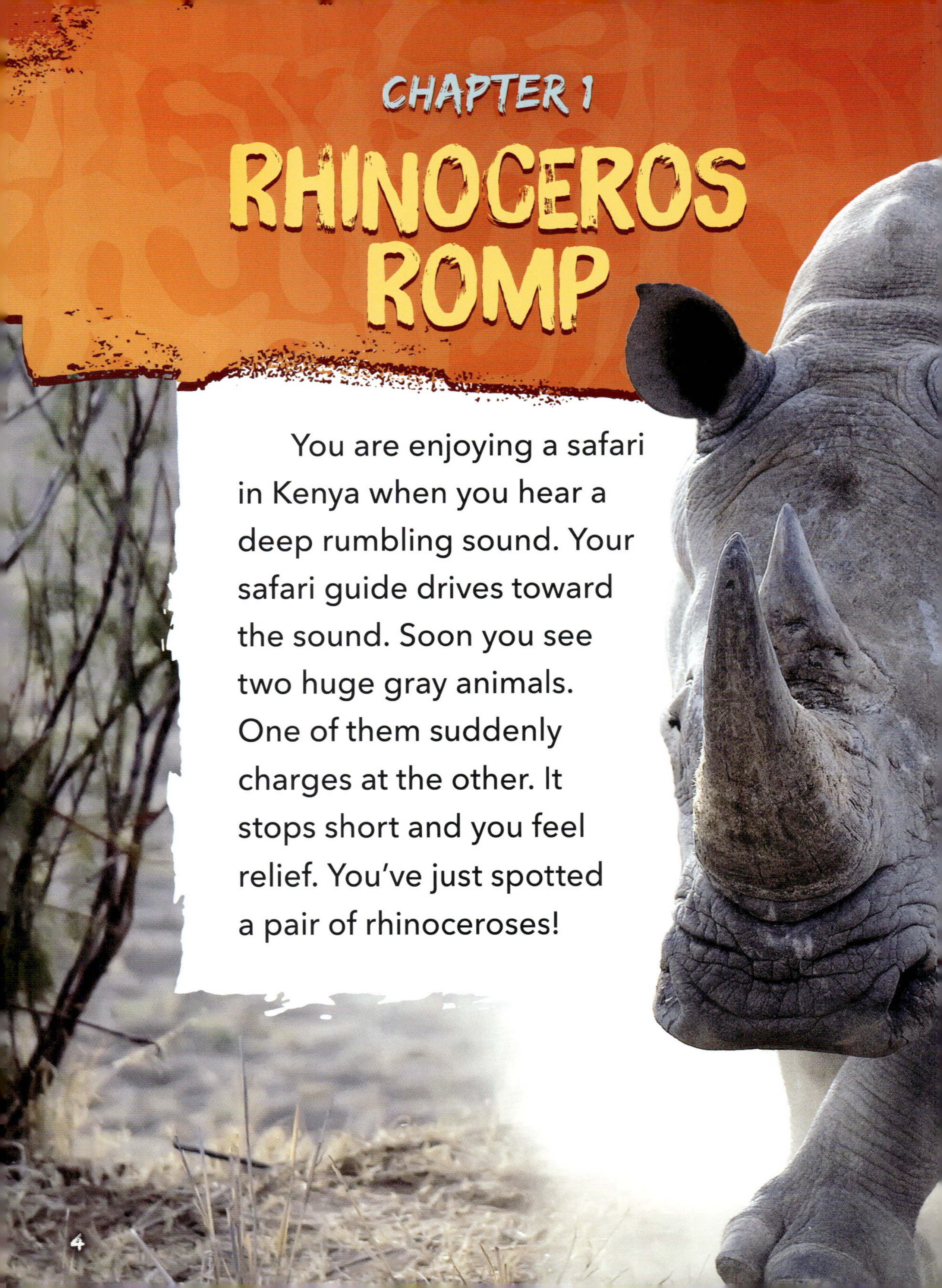

CHAPTER 1

RHINOCEROS ROMP

You are enjoying a safari in Kenya when you hear a deep rumbling sound. Your safari guide drives toward the sound. Soon you see two huge gray animals. One of them suddenly charges at the other. It stops short and you feel relief. You've just spotted a pair of rhinoceroses!

Rhinoceroses can run up to
30 miles per hour (48.3 kmh).

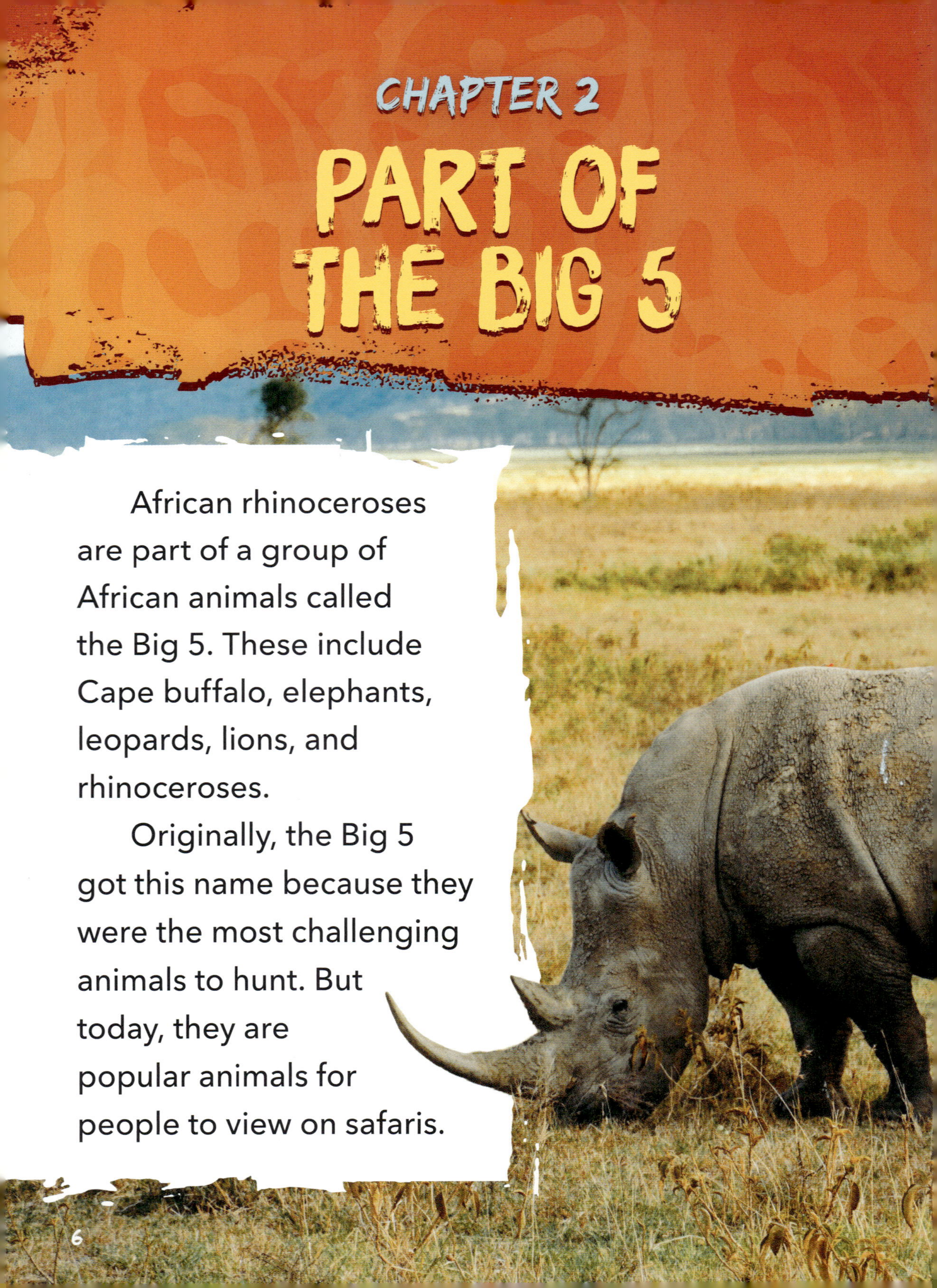

PART OF THE BIG 5

African rhinoceroses are part of a group of African animals called the Big 5. These include Cape buffalo, elephants, leopards, lions, and rhinoceroses.

Originally, the Big 5 got this name because they were the most challenging animals to hunt. But today, they are popular animals for people to view on safaris.

The word "rhinoceros" comes from the Greek words *rhino* and *ceros*. In English, these mean "nose horn."

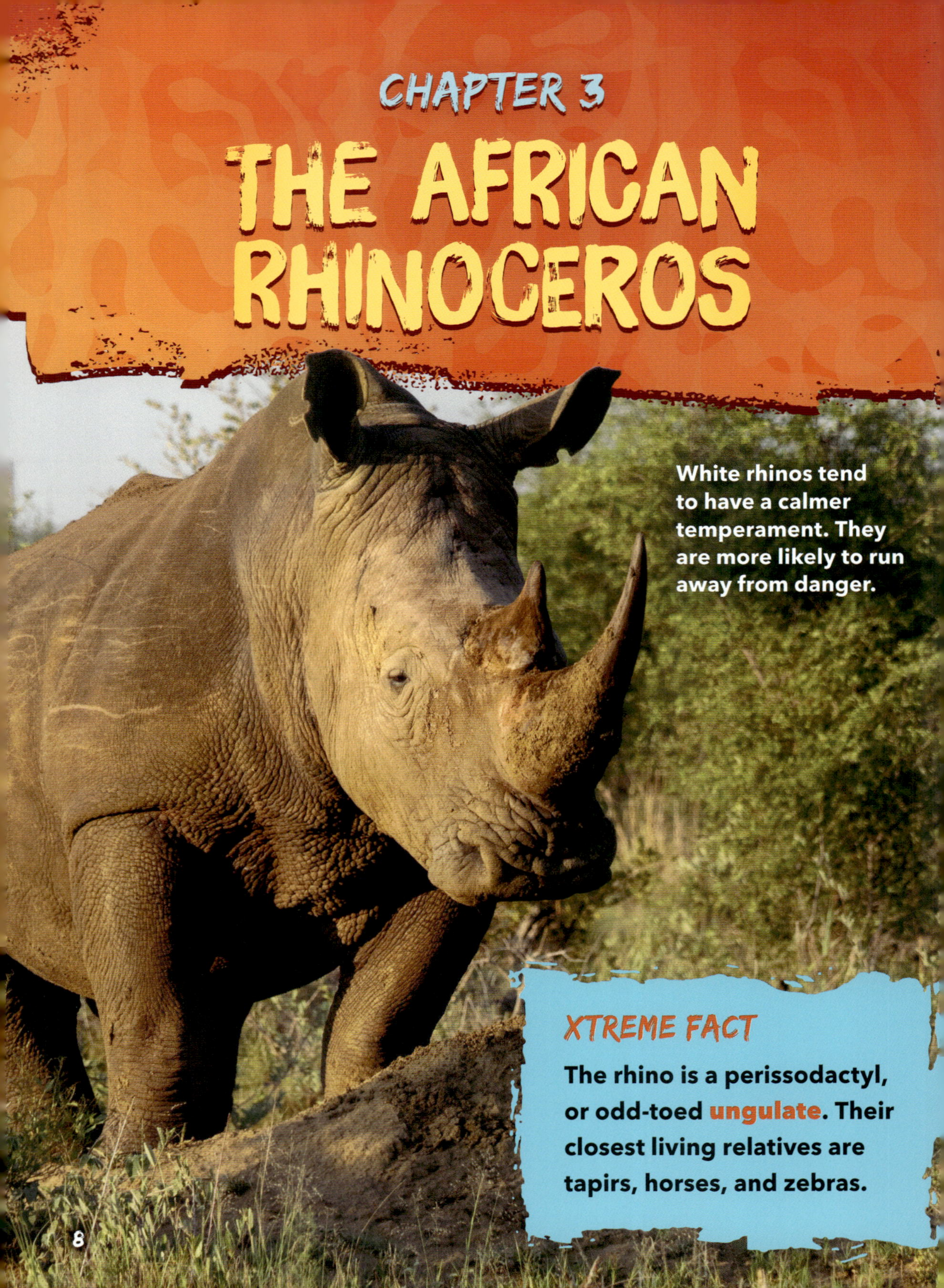
CHAPTER 3
THE AFRICAN RHINOCEROS

White rhinos tend to have a calmer temperament. They are more likely to run away from danger.

XTREME FACT

The rhino is a perissodactyl, or odd-toed ungulate. Their closest living relatives are tapirs, horses, and zebras.

There are two **species** of African rhinoceros or
rhino. They are the white rhino and the black rhino.
Both are gray in color. But they have some differences.
White rhinos have a square lip and long, tubelike ears.
Black rhinos have a rounder, pointed lip and smaller,
rounder ears.

The white rhino is the second-largest land animal. It stands up to seven feet (2 m) tall at the shoulder. It can weigh more than three tons (2.7 t).

The black rhino is smaller. It stands up to five feet (1.5 m) tall. It weighs up to one and a half tons (1.4 t).

White rhinos got their name
from the African word *wyd*.
Early explorers confused
wyd, which means "wide,"
with the word "white."

XTREME FACT

The longest recorded rhino horn was about five feet (1.5 m) long.

African rhinos have two horns. Rhino horns are made of keratin. Keratin is a **material** also found in human hair and nails. Rhinos use their horns to dig, protect themselves, and fight other rhinos.

African rhinos are almost completely hairless and have thick skin. A rhino's skin can be up to two inches (5.1 cm) thick. Rhinos also have poor eyesight. They mostly depend on their senses of hearing and smell.

Rhinos can move their ears independently. This means they can always have one ear pointed toward possible sounds of danger.

CHAPTER 4

LIFE AS A RHINO

African rhinos live on grasslands and **savannas**. Black rhinos live in eastern and southern Africa. They usually live alone.

White rhinos live in South Africa, Namibia, Zimbabwe, and Kenya. They may live in groups of up to 12 rhinos.

A group of rhinos is called a crash.

White rhinos can eat up
to 120 pounds (54 kg)
of grass each day.

Black and white rhinos are both **herbivores**. But they have different diets based on their **habitats**. Black rhinos live in areas with thick, woody plants. Their pointed lips help them eat branches, leaves, and fruit. White rhinos usually live in grassier areas. Their square lips help them eat grass.

A female rhino's **gestation** period is about 16 months long. Females have a calf every two to five years. They raise their calves for two to three years. Then the calves live on their own.

Rhinos give birth to
one calf at a time.

Rhinos mostly use scents to communicate. They mark their territories with **urine** and dung. They also use dung to identify other rhinos.

Rhinos also use vocal sounds to communicate. These include puffs, snorts, squeaks, screams, and more. They even make sounds on low **frequencies** that humans cannot hear.

Many rhinos will leave dung piles in the same spot. Other rhinos smell the dung to know which rhinos are in the area.

CHAPTER 5

RHINOS UNDER THREAT

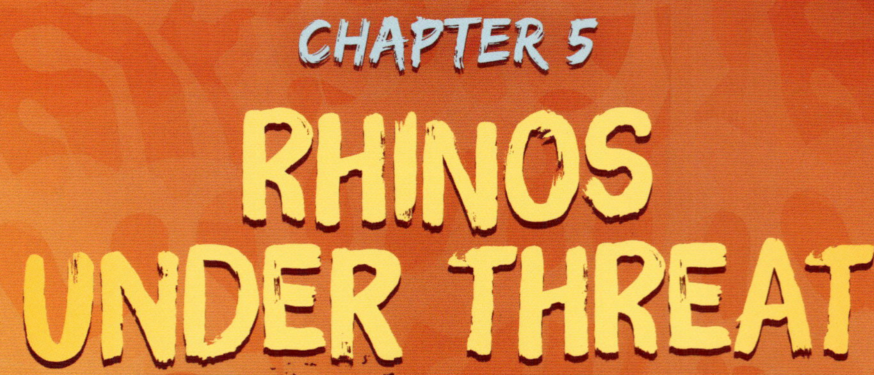

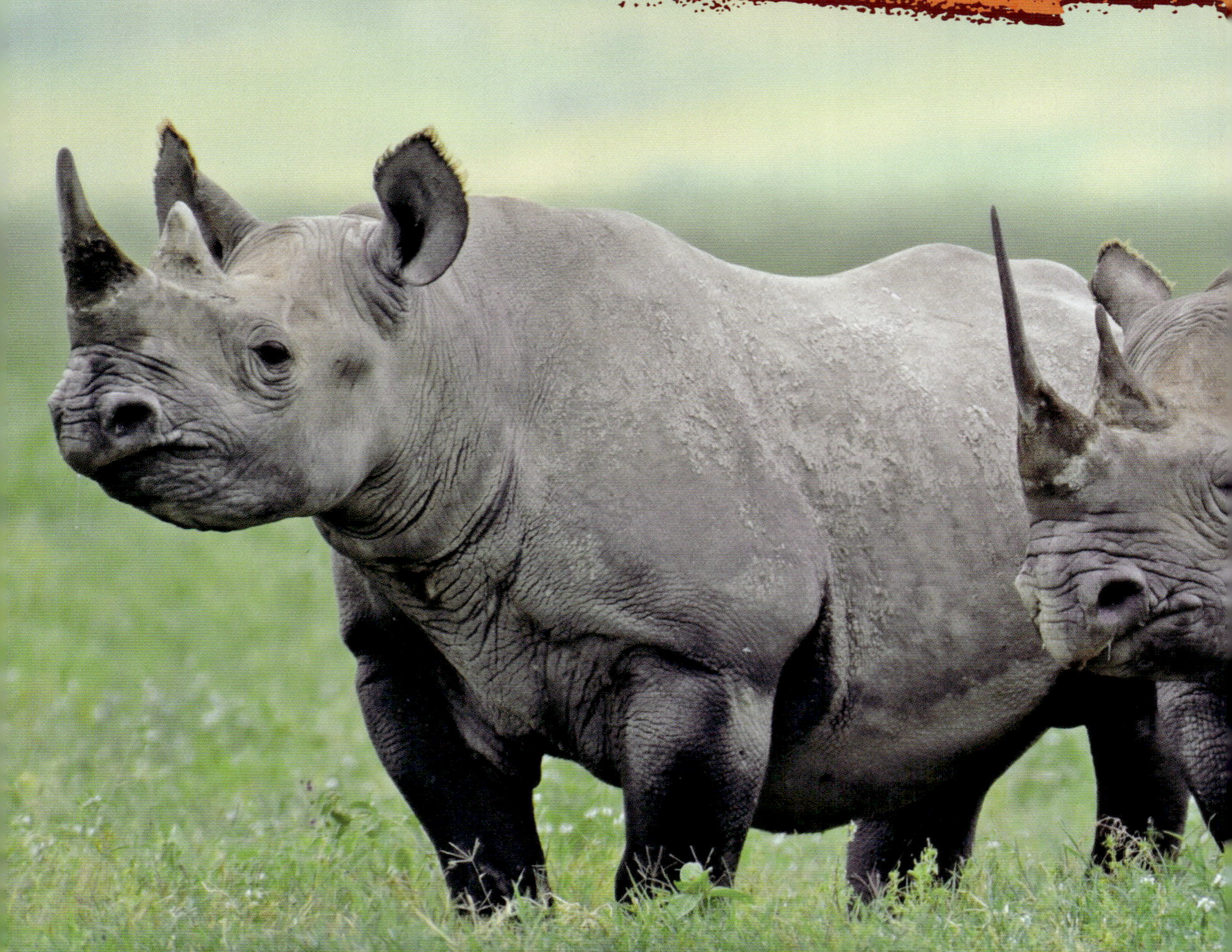

Almost all rhinos live in protected areas such as game reserves or national parks. Only some have been able to survive outside of these protected areas.

Black rhinos are critically endangered. This means the **species** is at the highest risk of becoming **extinct** in the wild. There are only about 6,000 adult black rhinos left in the wild.

In 2005, southern white rhinos were critically endangered.

White rhinos are near threatened. This means the **species** is likely to qualify as threatened in the **future**. There are about 17,000 adult white rhinos left in the wild.

There are two different types of white rhino. They are the northern and southern white rhino. In 2025, there were only two northern white rhinos left on Earth.

African rhinos face several threats. These include poaching and **habitat** loss and fragmentation. Poaching is illegal hunting. People poach rhinos for their horns.

Some people believe the horns have healing properties. Other people use rhino horns to make decorative knife handles. Trading rhino horns is illegal. But people still poach rhinos and trade rhino horns.

Due to poaching, the black rhino population dropped 96 percent between 1970 and 1990.

The land rhinos need is being taken over by the growth of human cities and farms.

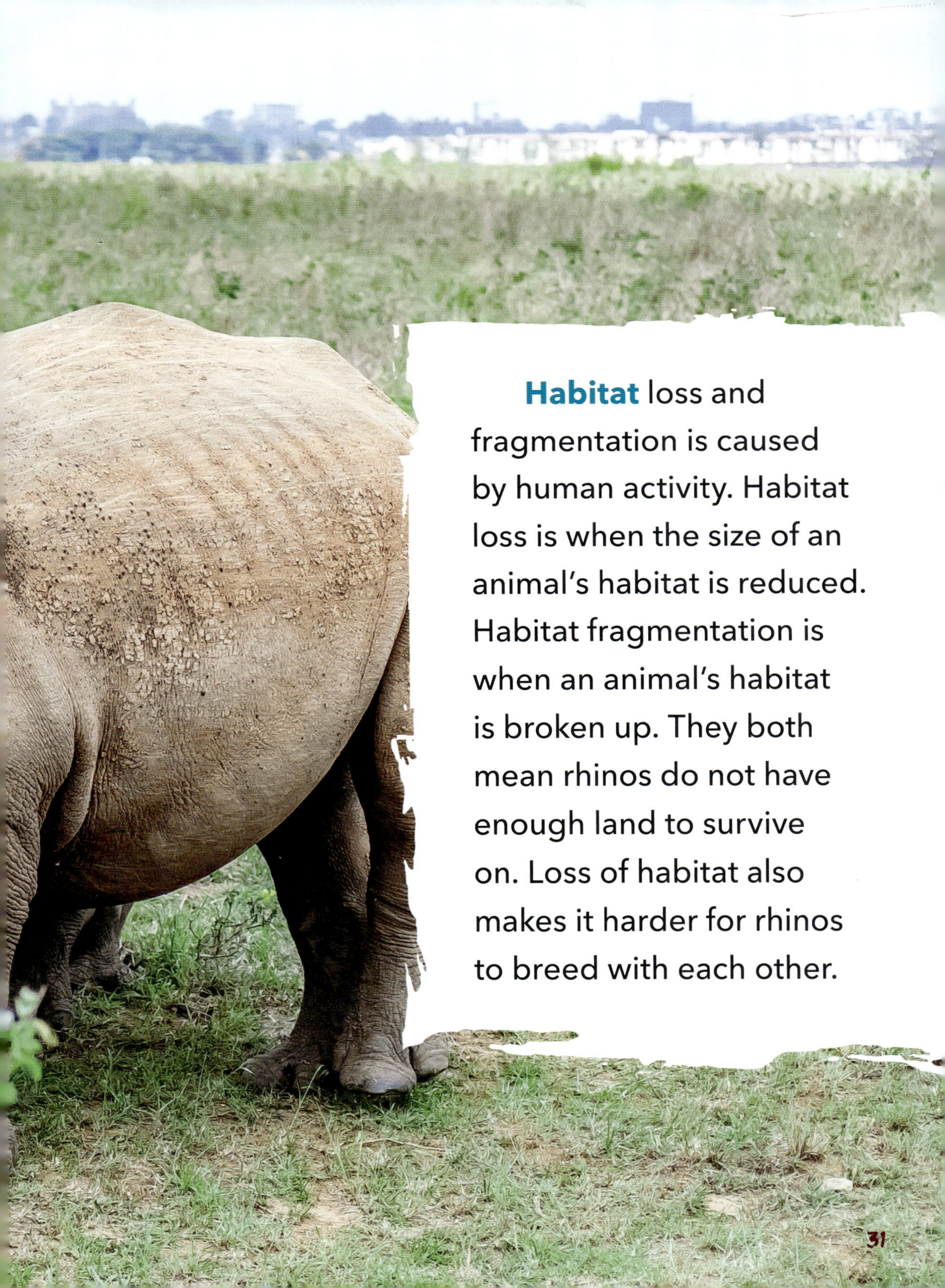

Habitat loss and fragmentation is caused by human activity. Habitat loss is when the size of an animal's habitat is reduced. Habitat fragmentation is when an animal's habitat is broken up. They both mean rhinos do not have enough land to survive on. Loss of habitat also makes it harder for rhinos to breed with each other.

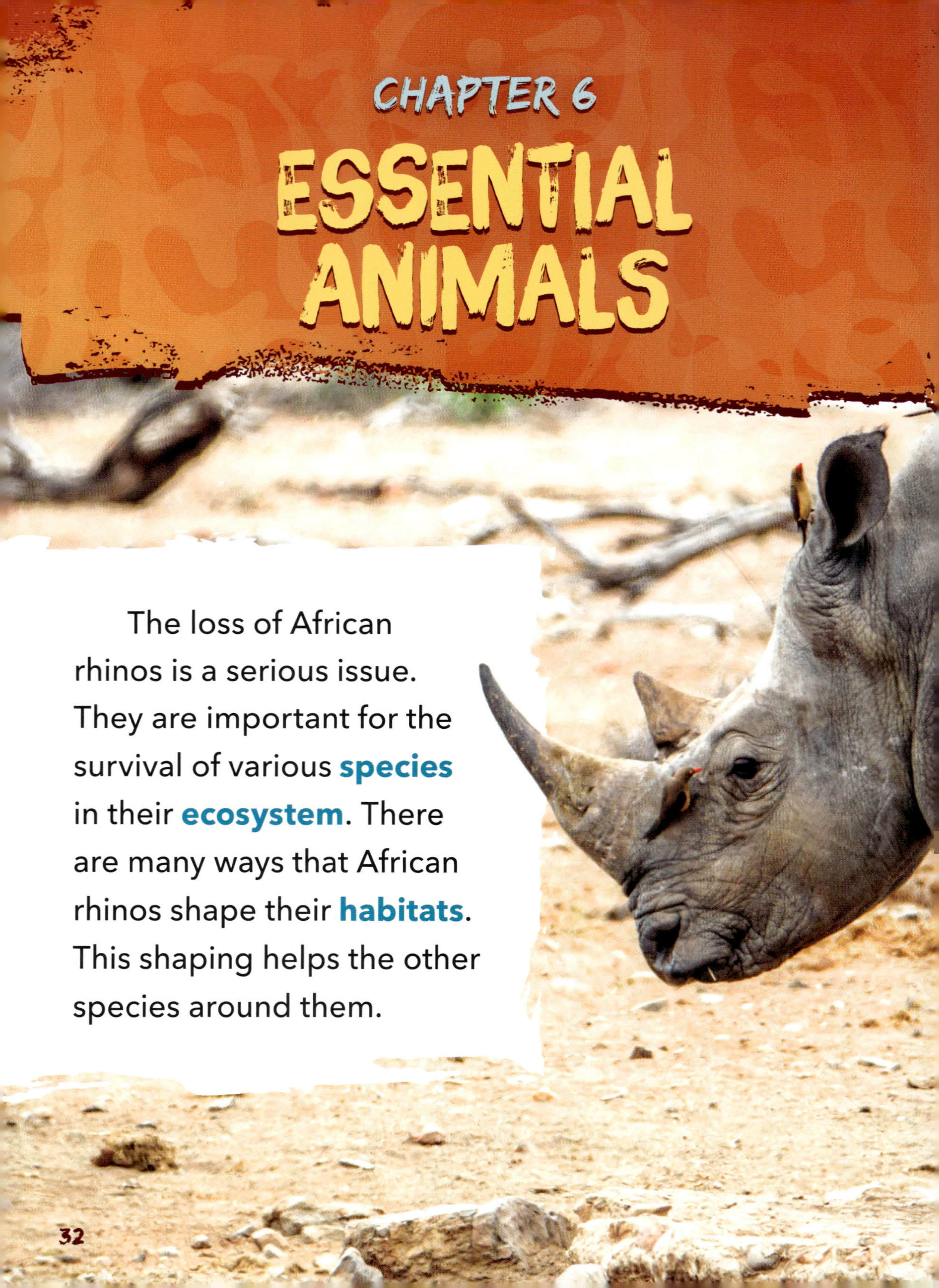

ESSENTIAL ANIMALS

The loss of African rhinos is a serious issue. They are important for the survival of various **species** in their **ecosystem**. There are many ways that African rhinos shape their **habitats**. This shaping helps the other species around them.

Oxpecker birds sit on rhinos and eat bugs off their skin. When they sense danger, oxpeckers will also make a loud call to warn the rhino.

Rhinos eat a lot of grass and
plants. This clears the way
for new plant growth.

Rhinos dig for water with their horns. This creates new watering holes for other animals. And when rhinos eat plants, they spread seeds through their dung. Their dung also provides the soil with **nutrients**. This helps new plants grow.

CHAPTER 7
HELP IS ON THE WAY
Some parks cut off rhinos' horns to stop poaching. But this also leads to rhinos moving around less because they don't have their horns for protection.

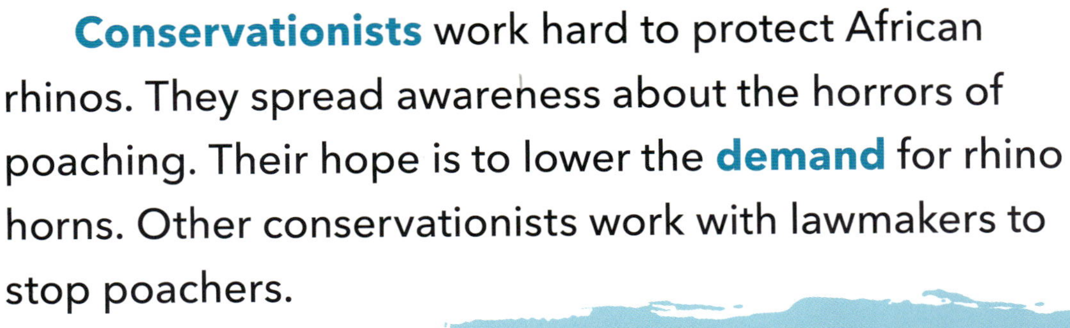

Conservationists work hard to protect African rhinos. They spread awareness about the horrors of poaching. Their hope is to lower the **demand** for rhino horns. Other conservationists work with lawmakers to stop poachers.

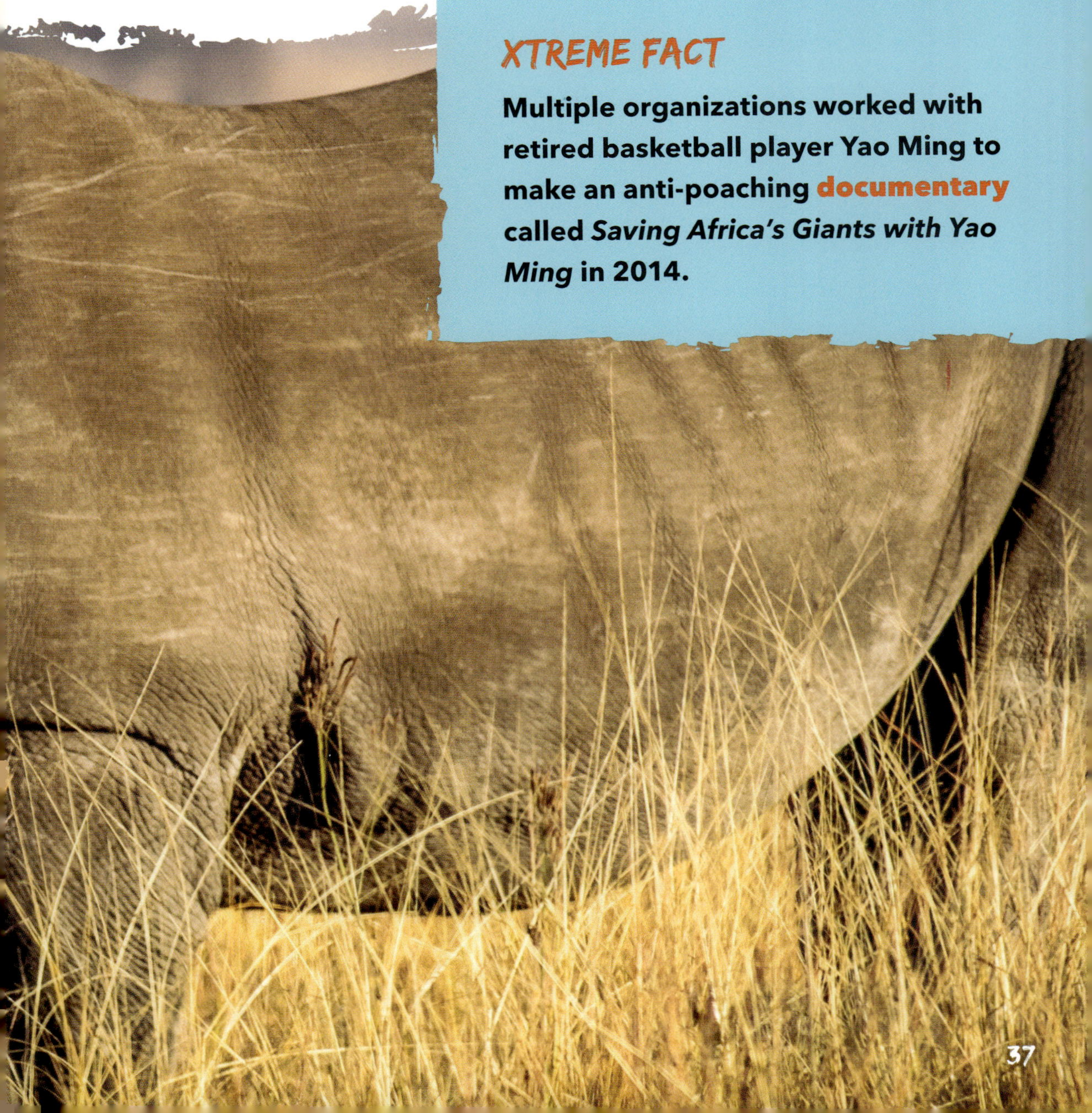

XTREME FACT

Multiple organizations worked with retired basketball player Yao Ming to make an anti-poaching documentary called *Saving Africa's Giants with Yao Ming* in 2014.

Many parks in Kenya
put microchips in
rhinos' horns. This
helps conservationists
track rhino movement
and protect these
animals from poaching.

Some organizations create and maintain rhino **sanctuaries**. These extra secure areas protect rhinos. The sanctuaries also protect other wildlife that are affected by poaching and **habitat** loss and fragmentation.

Other organizations work to increase the rhino population. They help move rhinos back to places where they once lived. This helps rhinos rebuild populations in their natural habitats.

CHAPTER 8

FAN FAVORITES

African rhinos are popular animals to view on safaris. They are exceptional and have many special features. People on safari might witness baby rhinos playing or adult rhinos **wallowing** in the mud. Rhinos are often more active at night when it is cooler. So, they can be more challenging to spot than some of the other Big 5 animals.

Rhinos will charge at anything they think is a threat. So it's important to keep a safe distance.

XTREME FACT

Conservationists are trying to use **in vitro fertilization** to produce a baby northern white rhino.

There are still many areas
to view rhinos on safari. The
Ol Pejeta Conservancy in Kenya
is home to the last two northern
white rhinos. Many black rhinos
also live there. National parks in
Kenya, Namibia, South Africa,
and Tanzania offer more
opportunities for rhino viewing.

CHAPTER 9

MORE TO EXPLORE

African rhinos are astonishing. Their size, horns, and thick skin make them stand out. Though rhinos face many threats, **conservationists** work hard to protect them and preserve their **habitats**. Animal lovers going on a wildlife safari might have a chance to see these remarkable creatures in their natural habitats.

African rhinos can live up to 40 years.

XTREME CHALLENGE

TAKE THE QUIZ BELOW AND
PUT WHAT YOU'VE LEARNED TO THE TEST!

1) What qualities make rhinos stand out?

2) What do rhinos use to communicate?

3) Why do people poach rhinos?

4) How are conservation organizations helping to reduce rhino poaching?

5) Would you want to see rhinos on a safari? Why or why not?

GLOSSARY

conservation—the planned management of natural resources or animals to protect them from damage or destruction. People who do this are conservationists.

demand—the amount of an available product that buyers are willing and able to purchase.

documentary—a film or television series that artistically presents facts.

ecosystem—a community of organisms and their surroundings.

extinct—no longer existing.

frequency—the number of waves, such as sound waves, passing a fixed point each second.

future—a time that has not yet occurred.

gestation—the carrying of a developing unborn baby in the uterus.

habitat—a place where a living thing is naturally found.

herbivore—an animal that eats only plants.

in vitro fertilization—a challenging set of procedures that can lead to pregnancy.

material—what a thing is made up of.

nutrient—a substance found in food and used in the body. Nutrients help the body grow, stay healthy, and repair itself.

sanctuary—a refuge for wildlife where predators are controlled and hunting is illegal.

savanna—a grassy plain with few or no trees.

species—a group of related living beings that can naturally produce offspring with each other.

ungulate—a plant-eating animal with four hooves. Ungulates include cows, deer, pigs, and horses.

urine—waste material produced by the kidneys.

wallow—to roll about in a lazy or relaxed way.

ONLINE RESOURCES

To learn more about African rhinoceroses, please visit **abdobooklinks.com** or scan this QR code. These links are routinely monitored and updated to provide the most current information available.

INDEX